The Amazing Silkworm

Monica Halpern

Silk

Have you ever seen or touched something made from silk? Silk is a strong thin thread that is used to make cloth. Silk cloth is soft to touch. It is strong, but it is also very light. Many beautiful things are made from silk, including clothing, furniture and curtains.

Silk clothing is soft to the touch and very light.

Silk is made from the long threads that come from an insect called a silkworm. The silkworm is a kind of moth. A silkworm moth is different from other moths because it is domesticated. This means it is raised by people. Very few silkworm moths live in the wild.

A silkworm crawls across a mulberry bush.

The Discovery of Silk

No one really knows how silk was discovered, but we do know that silk was first used in China. The Chinese learned what the silkworm could do more than 4,000 years ago.

A Chinese Tale

There is a very old Chinese story about how silk might have been discovered. In the story, a Chinese Empress first discovered silk thread when a strange oval object dropped into her teacup. When she tried to pull it out, the object unwound into a very long, shiny thread.

Silk thread is dyed many different bright colours before it is woven into clo

Chinese workers dyed silk threads by hand in the 1800s.

The Chinese dyed the silk threads many rich colours and wove them into cloth. Chinese traders sold some of the cloth to people from other countries. For a very long time, no one but the Chinese knew where silk came from. Who could imagine that an insect could make such beautiful cloth!

The Silkworm

Like all moths, the silkworm moth goes through four different stages of growth as it becomes an adult.

The four stages in the silkworm moth's life cycle are the egg, the caterpillar or larva, the pupa and the adult. The caterpillar stage is what we call the silkworm.

1 Egg

2 Caterpillar or larva

3 Pupa

4 Adult

The Egg

A female silkworm moth usually lays between 300 and 500 yellow eggs. Each egg is no bigger than the head of a pin. She sticks them onto a mulberry leaf one by one.

When the eggs hatch, tiny dark caterpillars emerge. They immediately eat their eggshells. Then, they begin to stuff themselves with the mulberry leaves on which they were born.

A silkworm moth lays its eggs on a mulberry leaf.

A tiny caterpillar hatches from its egg.

9

The Caterpillar

The young silkworm eats almost without stopping. It grows quickly and becomes very fat. After a few days, its skin starts to split. The caterpillar wiggles out of its old skin. The silkworm keeps eating mulberry leaves until it changes its skin again. This process is called moulting. The caterpillar moults four times.

After about four weeks, the silkworm is fully grown. It is now about seven-and-a-half centimetres long. It stops eating. It is ready to change into its adult form. It finds a quiet spot and begins to spin.

A silkworm caterpillar eats constantly.

These caterpillars are beginning to moult, or change their skins.

Pupa

The silkworm is making a cocoon. This is a covering to protect the silkworm from its enemies. As it spins, the silkworm moves its head back and forth. It spins one long, unbroken silken thread more than one-and-a-half kilometres long.

The silkworm works for two to three days making its cocoon. It works without stopping. When it is finished, the silkworm is completely enclosed in a thick, strong shell of silk thread.

Once inside its cocoon, the silkworm changes into a pupa. It sheds its skin for the last time.

A silkworm spins its cocoon on a mulberry leaf.

Inside its cocoon, a silkworm changes into a pupa.

13

Adult

Slowly, the pupa changes into an adult moth. After two weeks inside the cocoon, the silkworm moth is ready to come out. It produces a special liquid that dissolves the wall of the cocoon. Then, the silkworm moth pushes its way out of the cocoon. The life cycle is complete.

After two weeks, a silkworm moth emerges from its cocoon.

15

On silkworm farms, farmers harvest the silk at the pupa stage. Workers carefully unwind the long, delicate threads of the cocoon. They make spools of silk thread that are shipped to factories all over the world. There, the silk thread is woven into silk cloth.

A worker weaves silk thread into cloth.